Super Snacks

Table of Contents

Spicy Roasted Chickpeas

> 1 can (about 15 ounces) chickpeas, rinsed and drained
>
> 3 tablespoons olive oil
>
> ½ teaspoon salt
>
> ½ teaspoon black pepper
>
> ¾ to 1 tablespoon chili powder
>
> ⅛ to ¼ teaspoon ground red pepper
>
> 1 lime, cut into wedges

1. Preheat oven to 400°F.

2. Combine chickpeas, oil, salt and black pepper in large bowl. Spread in single layer on 15×10-inch jelly-roll pan.

3. Roast 15 minutes or until chickpeas begin to brown, shaking pan twice.

4. Sprinkle with chili powder and ground red pepper. Roast 5 minutes or until dark golden-red. Serve with lime wedges.

Makes 8 servings

Serving Size: ¼ cup
Calories 132, **Total Fat** 6g, **Saturated Fat** 1g,
Protein 3g, **Carbohydrate** 17g, **Cholesterol** 0mg,
Dietary Fiber 3g, **Sodium** 365mg

Dietary Exchanges: 1 Starch, 1 Fat

Classic Salsa

- 4 medium tomatoes, coarsely chopped
- 1 small onion, finely chopped
- 2 to 3 jalapeño peppers or serrano peppers,* seeded and minced
- ¼ cup chopped fresh cilantro
- 1 small clove garlic, minced
- 2 tablespoons lime juice
- ⅛ teaspoon salt (optional)
- ⅛ teaspoon black pepper (optional)

Jalapeño and serrano peppers can sting and irritate the skin, so wear rubber gloves when handling peppers and do not touch your eyes.

Combine tomatoes, onion, jalapeños, cilantro, garlic and lime juice in medium bowl. Add salt and black pepper, if desired. Cover and refrigerate at least 1 hour before serving.*   *Makes 2½ cups (about 20 servings)*

Salsa can be made up to 3 days in advance to allow flavors to develop.

Serving Size: 2 tablespoons
Calories 8, **Total Fat** 1g, **Saturated Fat** 1g,
Protein 1g, **Carbohydrate** 2g, **Cholesterol** 0mg,
Dietary Fiber 1g, **Sodium** 3mg

Dietary Exchanges: Free

Superfoods Smoothie

  1 cup coarsely chopped kale

  1 cup baby spinach

  1 cup ice

  1 banana

  ½ cup low-calorie apple juice cocktail

1. Combine all ingredients in blender or food processor; blend until smooth and well blended.

2. Pour into glass. Serve immediately.

Makes 1 serving

Calories 155, **Total Fat** 1g, **Saturated Fat** 0g, **Protein** 4g, **Carbohydrate** 37g, **Cholesterol** 0mg, **Dietary Fiber** 5g, **Sodium** 59mg

Dietary Exchanges: 1½ Fruit

Crisp Oats Trail Mix

- 1 cup old-fashioned oats
- ½ cup unsalted toasted pumpkin seeds (pepitas)
- ½ cup dried cranberries
- ½ cup raisins
- 2 tablespoons maple syrup
- 1 teaspoon canola oil
- ½ teaspoon ground cinnamon
- ¼ teaspoon salt

1. Preheat oven to 325°F. Line baking sheet with heavy-duty foil.

2. Combine all ingredients in large bowl; mix well. Spread on prepared baking sheet.

3. Bake 20 minutes or until oats are lightly browned, stirring halfway through. Cool completely on baking sheet. Store in airtight container.

Makes 2½ cups (about 10 servings)

Serving Size: ¼ cup
Calories 123, **Total Fat** 5g, **Saturated Fat** 1g,
Protein 3g, **Carbohydrate** 20g, **Cholesterol** 0mg,
Dietary Fiber 2g, **Sodium** 60mg

Dietary Exchanges: 1 Starch, 1 Fat

Double Berry Pops

2 cups plain nonfat Greek yogurt, divided

1 cup blueberries

3 tablespoons sugar, divided

6 (5-ounce) paper or plastic cups or pop molds

1 cup sliced strawberries

6 pop sticks

1. Combine 1 cup yogurt, blueberries and 1½ tablespoons sugar in blender or food processor; blend until smooth.

2. Pour mixture into cups. Freeze 2 hours.

3. Combine strawberries, remaining 1 cup yogurt and 1½ tablespoons sugar in blender or food processor; blend until smooth.

4. Pour mixture over blueberry layer in cups . Cover top of each cup with small piece of foil. Freeze 2 hours.

5. Insert sticks through center of foil. Freeze 4 hours or until firm.

6. To serve, remove foil and peel away paper cups or gently twist frozen pops out of plastic cups.   *Makes 6 pops*

Serving Size: 1 pop
Calories 90, **Total Fat** 0g, **Saturated Fat** 0g,
Protein 7g, **Carbohydrate** 15g, **Cholesterol** 0mg,
Dietary Fiber 1g, **Sodium** 30mg

Dietary Exchanges: ½ Starch, ½ Fruit, ½ Meat

Super Nachos

12 baked reduced-fat tortilla chips (about 1½ ounces)

½ cup (2 ounces) shredded reduced-fat Cheddar cheese

¼ cup fat-free refried beans

2 tablespoons chunky salsa

Microwave Directions

1. Arrange chips in single layer on large microwavable plate. Sprinkle with cheese.

2. Spoon 1 teaspoon beans over each chip; top with ½ teaspoon salsa.

3. Microwave on MEDIUM (50 %) 1½ minutes;* rotate dish. Microwave 1 to 1½ minutes or until cheese is melted. *Makes 4 servings*

If using a microwave with a turntable, nachos should be ready to eat at this point.

Note: To make the nachos in the oven, preheat oven to 350°F. Line baking sheet with foil. Assemble nachos on prepared baking sheet as directed above. Bake 10 to 12 minutes or until cheese is melted.

Serving Size: 3 nachos
Calories 82, **Total Fat** 4g, **Saturated Fat** 3g,
Protein 4g, **Carbohydrate** 7g, **Cholesterol** 10mg,
Dietary Fiber 1g, **Sodium** 263mg

Dietary Exchanges: ½ Starch, ½ Fat, ½ Meat

Peanut Butter Cereal Bars

  - 3 cups mini marshmallows
  - 3 tablespoons butter or margarine
  - ½ cup reduced-fat peanut butter
  - 3½ cups crisp rice cereal
  - 1 cup quick oats
  - ⅓ cup mini semisweet chocolate chips

Microwave Directions

1. Spray 13×9-inch baking pan with nonstick cooking spray.

2. Combine marshmallows and butter in large microwavable bowl. Microwave on HIGH 15 seconds; stir. Microwave 1 minute; stir until marshmallows are melted and mixture is smooth. Add peanut butter; stir. Add cereal and oats; stir until well coated. Spread into prepared pan. Immediately sprinkle with chocolate chips; lightly press into cereal mixture.

3. Cool completely in pan before cutting and serving.   *Makes 40 bars*

tip To make spreading the cereal mixture easier and cleanup a snap, lightly spray your spoon with nonstick cooking spray before stirring these bars.

Serving Size: 1 bar
Calories 66, **Total Fat** 3g, **Saturated Fat** 1g,
Protein 1g, **Carbohydrate** 10g, **Cholesterol** 2mg,
Dietary Fiber 1g, **Sodium** 54mg

Dietary Exchanges: ½ Starch, ½ Fat

Mediterranean Tuna Cups

- 3 English cucumbers
- ⅔ cup plain nonfat Greek yogurt
- ⅓ cup coarsely chopped pitted kalamata olives
- ⅓ cup finely chopped red onion
- 2 tablespoons fresh lemon juice
- ¼ teaspoon garlic salt
- 2 cans (5 ounces each) solid white albacore tuna in water, drained and flaked

  Thinly sliced red bell pepper (optional)

1. Cut ends off of each cucumber; cut each cucumber into 10 slices. Scoop out cucumber slices with a rounded ½ teaspoon, leaving thick shell.

2. Stir yogurt, olives, onion, lemon juice and garlic salt in large bowl until smooth and well blended. Stir in tuna.

3. Spoon about 1 tablespoon tuna salad into each cucumber cup. Serve immediately. Garnish with bell pepper.   *Makes 30 cups (about 10 servings)*

Serving Size: 3 tuna cups
Calories 32, **Total Fat** 1g, **Saturated Fat** 0g,
Protein 5g, **Carbohydrate** 2g, **Cholesterol** 8mg,
Dietary Fiber 1g, **Sodium** 102mg

Dietary Exchanges: 1 Meat

Sweet and Savory Onion Dip

1 tablespoon olive oil

3 onions, diced

2 cups plain low-fat Greek yogurt

¼ cup grated Parmesan cheese

2 tablespoons fresh lemon juice

⅛ teaspoon ground red pepper

Vegetable sticks, crackers and/or chips

1. Heat oil in large nonstick skillet over medium-high heat. Add onions; cook and stir 6 to 8 minutes or until golden brown. Reduce heat to low; cook 15 minutes or until onions are deep golden brown; stirring occasionally.

2. Meanwhile, stir yogurt, cheese, lemon juice and ground red pepper in large bowl until smooth and well blended.

3. Stir onions into yogurt mixture. Cover and refrigerate at least 2 hours before serving. Serve with vegetable sticks, crackers and/or chips.

Makes 3 cups (about 24 servings)

Serving Size: 2 tablespoons
Calories 28, **Total Fat** 1g, **Saturated Fat** 1g,
Protein 2g, **Carbohydrate** 2g, **Cholesterol** 3mg,
Dietary Fiber 1g, **Sodium** 22mg

Dietary Exchanges: Free

Crisp & Crunchy Rosemary Flats

½ cup all-purpose flour

½ cup whole wheat flour

1 tablespoon chopped fresh rosemary

½ teaspoon baking powder

½ teaspoon salt

¼ cup water

2 tablespoons plus 1 teaspoon olive oil, divided

1 tablespoon shredded Parmesan cheese

1. Preheat oven to 450°F. Place baking sheet in oven.

2. Combine flours, rosemary, baking powder and salt in medium bowl; mix well. Stir in water and 2 tablespoons oil until dough forms.

3. Knead dough on floured surface into ball. Divide dough into 4 balls. Roll out each ball into oval shape, about ⅛ inch thick.

4. Remove baking sheet from oven. Place dough pieces on baking sheet. Pierce tops with fork. Brush with remaining 1 teaspoon oil; sprinkle evenly with cheese.

5. Bake 12 to 15 minutes or until edges are browned. Let stand 5 to 10 minutes to cool slightly. Break into pieces; serve warm or cool completely.

Makes 4 servings

Calories 184, **Total Fat** 9g, **Saturated Fat** 1g, **Protein** 4g, **Carbohydrate** 23g, **Cholesterol** 1mg, **Dietary Fiber** 2g, **Sodium** 374mg

Dietary Exchanges: 1½ Starch, 1½ Fat

Kale Chips

    1 large bunch kale (about 1 pound)

    1 to 2 tablespoons olive oil

    1 teaspoon garlic salt or other seasoned salt

1. Preheat oven to 350°F. Line baking sheets with parchment paper.

2. Wash kale and pat dry with paper towels. Remove center ribs and stems; discard. Cut leaves into 2- to 3-inch-wide pieces.

3. Combine leaves, oil and garlic salt in large bowl; toss to coat. Spread onto prepared baking sheets.

4. Bake 10 to 15 minutes or until edges are lightly browned and leaves are crisp.* Cool completely on baking sheets. Store in airtight container.

Makes 6 servings

If the leaves are lightly browned but not crisp, turn oven off and let chips stand in oven until crisp, about 10 minutes. Do not keep the oven on as the chips will burn easily.

Calories 43, **Total Fat** 3g, **Saturated Fat** 1g, **Protein** 2g, **Carbohydrate** 5g, **Cholesterol** 0mg, **Dietary Fiber** 1g, **Sodium** 180mg

Dietary Exchanges: ½ Fat, 1 Vegetable

Berry Bran Muffins

    2 cups dry bran cereal
    1¼ cups fat-free (skim) milk
    ½ cup packed brown sugar
    1 egg, lightly beaten
    ¼ cup vegetable oil
    1 teaspoon vanilla
    1¼ cups all-purpose flour
    1 tablespoon baking powder
    ¼ teaspoon salt
    1 cup fresh or frozen blueberries (partially thawed if frozen)

1. Preheat oven to 350°F. Line 12 standard (2½-inch) muffin cups with paper baking cups.

2. Combine cereal and milk in medium bowl. Let stand 5 minutes to soften. Add brown sugar, egg, oil and vanilla; beat until well blended. Combine flour, baking powder and salt in large bowl. Stir into cereal mixture just until dry ingredients are moistened. Gently fold in berries. Spoon evenly into prepared muffin cups.

3. Bake 20 to 25 minutes (25 to 30 if using frozen berries) or until toothpick inserted into centers comes out clean. Serve warm.   *Makes 12 muffins*

Serving Size: 1 muffin
Calories 172, **Total Fat** 5g, **Saturated Fat** 1g,
Protein 4g, **Carbohydrate** 29g, **Cholesterol** 18mg,
Dietary Fiber 4g, **Sodium** 287mg

Dietary Exchanges: 2 Starch, 1 Fat

Mediterranean-Style Deviled Eggs

¼ cup finely diced cucumber

¼ cup finely diced tomato

2 teaspoons fresh lemon juice

⅛ teaspoon salt

6 hard-cooked eggs, peeled and sliced in half lengthwise

⅓ cup roasted garlic or any flavor hummus

Chopped fresh parsley (optional)

1. Combine cucumber, tomato, lemon juice and salt in small bowl; gently mix.

2. Remove yolks from eggs; discard. Spoon 1 heaping teaspoon hummus into each egg half. Top with ½ teaspoon cucumber-tomato mixture and parsley, if desired. Serve immediately. *Makes 6 servings*

Serving Size: 2 filled egg halves
Calories 49, **Total Fat** 3g, **Saturated Fat** 0g,
Protein 4g, **Carbohydrate** 3g, **Cholesterol** 0mg,
Dietary Fiber 1g, **Sodium** 157mg

Dietary Exchanges: 1 Meat

Pear-Topped Grahams

¼ cup light cream cheese

8 cinnamon graham cracker squares

4 teaspoons raspberry fruit spread

1 pear, halved, cored and cut into 16 slices

Spread 1 tablespoon cream cheese over each whole cracker. Spoon ½ teaspoon fruit spread on top. Arrange 4 pear slices on top of each cracker, overlapping slightly. Serve immediately. *Makes 4 servings*

Serving Size: 1 graham
Calories 127, **Total Fat** 4g, **Saturated Fat** 2g, **Protein** 3g, **Carbohydrate** 21g, **Cholesterol** 10mg, **Dietary Fiber** 2g, **Sodium** 127mg

Dietary Exchanges: 1 Starch, 1 Fat